I AM!

EVERY GIRL NEEDS TO KNOW WHO SHE IS

By MICHELLIAH MCCRANEY

I Am! Every Girl Needs to Know Who She Is
Copyright © 2017 by Michelliah McCraney

ISBN: 978-0998101309

Empyrion Publishing
PO Box 784327
Winter Garden FL 34778
info@EmpyrionPublishing.com

All rights reserved. No part of this book may be reproduced, stored in a retrieval system, or transmitted in any form or by any means – electronic, mechanical, photocopy, recording, or any other, without permission in writing from the author.

Photo credits:

Cover Page – basheeradesigns©123rf.com
Page 8 & 15 – poznyakov©123rf.com
Page 14 - photojog©123rf.com
Page 16 - petro©123rf.com
Page 17 - bykobrinphoto©123rf.com
Page 21 - pat138241©123rf.com
Page 27 - stockbrocker©123rf.com
Page 33 - creatista©123rf.com
Page 38 - bubutu©123rf.com
Page 40 – studiom1©123rf.com

Printed in the United States of America

I AM!

EDUCATING! EQUIPPING! EMPOWERING! GIRLS

Builds: *Character and Confidence*

Eliminates: *Identity Crisis, Peer Pressure, Bullying, and Low Self-Esteem*

Teaches: *Moral Values, Social Skills, and Self-Respect*

Encourages: *Health and Wellness*

Empowers: *Girls to have Faith*

I AM! Series by Michelliah McCraney:

I AM! EVERY GIRL NEEDS TO KNOW WHO SHE IS
I AM! 10 TRUTHS TO HELP GIRLS KNOW WHO THEY ARE
I AM! FUN AND INTERESTING FACTS ABOUT GIRLS FROM CHILDHOOD TO ADULTHOOD
and
I AM! ALL-IN-ONE WORKBOOK AND JOURNAL

Ms. McCraney has written a very fun book that will educate, empower and equip girls to embrace their authentic self.

Dr. Rosalind Osgood
Chair, Broward County School Board

*Wow! Where was this book when I was growing up? Not only is this a GREAT tool for my 13-year-old daughter, Tiffany, but **I AM!** definitely grabbing copies for my 25-year-old daughter, Mychaela and each one of my NBA son's daughters as well. The illustrations make it inviting and easy to read and I love that it shows a variety of young ladies that reflect the real world. KUDOS to you Michelliah! Thank you for being such a positive example to females of ALL ages.*

Fatima A. Smith, Mother of 5 stars, including NBA forward Michael Beasley Business Owner & Mentor

Wow! This is an amazing affirmation of the beauty, strength, and talents of girls! Girls of all nationalities can take from these pages a message of pride that will shape their ascent into womanhood. Michelliah McCraney's passion for mentoring and supporting young women is evident in this three part series. She has developed a great resource for girls of all ages on their way to self-discovery.

Nacole S. Guyton, Ed. S, Curriculum Supervisor

To my Father in heaven who allowed me to be broken, in order to be made better. Thank you for making me the virtuous woman I AM

To my daughter: Marquitta. Thank you for motherhood.

To my granddaughters: Taylor and D'Shari.

Thank you for all I have to look forward to.

To my sister Joeann (1958-Eternity).

To my mother, sisters, and host of nieces.

To my dad, you made my childhood memories special and left me with a foundation that has everything to do with who I Am today.

Thank you for allowing me to be a part of your journey and for being a part of mine.

Dear Reader,

Every girl's upbringing and experiences are different. Some girls may have a mentor, older sister, or positive role models in their lives that they can talk to or go to for help or advice and others may not.

Some girls may be able to say that they come from a loving home or environment with a parent or guardian that cares and takes the time to teach her some of the things she will get from reading this book. But other girls may not have such experience. Regardless of which girl you may be, you are important to me.

Therefore, I would like for every girl that reads this book to embrace it as a guide and friend, which is similar to having a mentor. The first important thing I want you to know is there will never be anyone or anything more attractive than knowing who you are.

Others will try to convince you to become something that you are not. Some will even go as far as to tell you what they want you to be and try to steer you in that direction. But when you develop into your own person and know who you are, the opinions, plots, and plans of others will not matter to you.

Before you can ever genuinely embrace anything or anyone, you will have to first embrace the number one person in your life, and that is you. Everything about you (including your beliefs and desires) starts inside and flows outside.

That is why every girl deserves to be told who she is at a very young age. I believe that reading or hearing the things in this book will empower you throughout your growth process. If you read or hear them often enough, even if you stray away, they will never leave you.

A Prayer for Every Girl Who Reads this Book:

Heavenly Father, please smile on this young lady.

Let her be empowered by the words You have given me to write in this book.

Help her to see herself through these words. Help her to love herself unconditionally.

Increase her confidence and strengthen her where she may be weak.

Through this book please build her character and fix any low self-esteem issues she may have. Show her what gifts she possesses and everything you intend for her to be.

Tell her who she is, and when she learns who she really is, help her to never forget. Help her to set standards and goals for herself that are achievable and that are not centered on her peers or any young-man.

Give her power to say no when necessary and courage to do the right thing when she doesn't feel like it.

If she is hurting or having a hard time in any area of her mind, body or spirit, heal her.

If she is confused or feels neglected, restore her. If she is lost, secure her and bring her to safety. If she needs change, transform her.

If she has ever walked with her head down, been picked on, felt like she doesn't fit in, or been abused, I ask that You make her to walk with her head held high, and cause her to never be afraid of, or bullied by another creature from this day forth.

And lastly, Lord, when she comes to the end and closes this book, I ask that You give her peace and that You would continue to meet her every need.

AMEN.

21 Reasons Why Every Girl Needs to Know Who She Is

Not knowing who you are causes you to want to be like someone else rather than yourself.

Not knowing who you are causes you to doubt that you can do what you are more than capable of doing.

Not knowing who you are causes you to act in a way that is not within your character, just to fit in.

Not knowing who you are causes you to compare yourself to others.

Not knowing who you are causes you to depend on your peers or others to approve of you.

Not knowing who you are causes you to become a follower and not a leader.

Not knowing who you are causes you to struggle with low self-esteem.

Not knowing who you are causes you to feel inferior to others.

Not knowing who you are causes you to think and feel that you are invaluable and unworthy of love.

Not knowing who you are causes you to feel like your life is hopeless or useless.

Not knowing who you are makes you think you are not pretty.

Not knowing who you are makes you unhappy or dissatisfied with who you are.

Not knowing who you are makes you uncertain about what you want to be.

Not knowing who you are causes you to envy or to become jealous hearted toward others.

Not knowing who you are causes you to lack confidence.

Not knowing who you are causes you to feel depressed.

Not knowing who you are allows you to settle for less than the best.

Not knowing who you are can result in wrongdoing and many regrets.

Not knowing who you are prevents you from loving yourself.

Not knowing who you are can prevent you from recognizing your potential.

Not knowing who you are can prevent you from fulfilling your dreams.

Knowing Who You Are

Knowing who you are is one of the most important things you will accomplish in life. It can also be one of the most interesting discoveries you'll ever make.

And I cannot think of a better person to know than YOU, or a better time than now to begin, while you are yet still young with lots and lots of growing and learning to do.

WHO ARE YOU?

I AM! A FLOWER

I BLOSSOM

But first, I must be watered, fertilized, and nurtured.

Then I GROW! GROW! GROW!

I grow from a little girl to a young lady and into womanhood.

I AM in different SIZES, SHAPES, and COLORS.

I stretch my arms instead of my wings to go where

I want to go and do what I want to do.

I FLY! I am COLORFUL and

as FREE as a BUTTERFLY!

I AM!

Girl, female, & soon to be woman.

POETICALLY SPEAKING:

I AM!

A GIRL, IN MY OWN WORLD

I AM AS VALUABLE AND EXPENSIVE

AS A PIECE OF JEWELRY

LIKE A RUBY, DIAMOND, OR PEARL.

KNOWING WHO I AM MAKES ME AN ASSET

THROUGHOUT

THE WORLD AND TO EVERY RACE OF GIRLS.

I AM! DESTINED

Purpose lives on the inside of me. I know this because destiny is constantly leading and guiding me.

It speaks to me about where I should go, what I should do and even about the things I desire to be and the person I should always thrive to become.

It doesn't allow me to give up or give in. As a matter of fact it is the reason I awake determined to fight to the end, determined to stand until I win.

Looking at the distance can sometime be fearful, but because I know I am destined I'm not doubtful.

For there is a plan for my life according to Jeremiah 29:11 in the bible, and that makes me powerful.

Therefore, I take my steps, forget about everything else, and keep my eyes focused on the source and the strength. For, He is my help!

One Day You Will Be Asked This Question, and When You Are, You Don't Want to Have to Think About It WHAT ARE YOU?

I AM patient. I wait my turn. In school I raise my hand and patiently wait to be noticed and called upon.

It is not necessary for me to make noises or blurt out to be seen.

I do not skip others. I can walk in a line without fighting or arguing about whose first or wanting to be first.

I AM positive. I look for the good in everybody and in every situation.

I AM gifted. I possess (own) at least one gift (talent).

I AM strong. "I can do all things through Christ who strengthens me" (Philippians 4:13).

I AM courageous. I have the courage to do things that others do not.

I AM hopeful. I always hope for the best.

I AM blessed. I have something that someone else does not, and wish they did.

I AM respectful. I respect my mind, body, and spirit. When I am being spoken to by an adult, I answer, "Yes, m'am," "No, m'am," "Yes, sir," or, "No, sir." I carry myself in the most respectable way possible.

I AM a light in this world. I am a light within my home, family, community, school, church, and everywhere I go. Matthew 5:14-16 in the Bible tells me so.

I AM salt. I add flavor to everything I touch. Matthew 5:13 proves I am such.

There is nothing meaningless about my life. I have what I need and what it takes to fulfill my purpose here on earth.

I have no reason to be jealous or envious of anyone.

I AM fearfully and wonderfully made!

I AM!

A piece of a puzzle

I am the result of someone's prayer and

the answer to someone's question.

I am special! I am a dream come true!

I AM!

A Book

I have a story that has a beginning and an end.

My footprints will continue to make new beginnings and friends, as my heart loves and breaks, yet continues to mend.

I AM!

A spoken language

Not a broken language. I speak one or more of the world languages like English, Spanish, Creole, Patwa, or Portuguese.

I speak when I am spoken to and answer when I am asked a question.

I pronounce my words properly and make myself clear. I am a verbal expression with a voice and an opinion.

I speak with authority because I've been given Dominion!

I AM!

One or more of the colors in the rainbow

I am a reflection of history. I am culture and color, freedom, justice and equality.

I am black, white, brown, purple, green, blue, red or yellow.

I help to make the world colorful and mellow.

I am the shade and the sunlight, in every "day and night."

I add beauty and life, to the stars surrounding the moonlight.

I am radiant (brilliant), in God's sight!

I AM!

I AM

ME, MYSELF, AND I

I AM JUST WHAT I LIKE.

I AM A TOUCH OF THIS

AND A TOUCH OF THAT,

WHICH MAKES ME

JUST RIGHT!

"I AM! A SONG"

I AM a melody; a harmony

I AM pop, rap, blues, rhythm, hip hop, and soul.

I AM praise and worship.

I AM the tune in the sounds of a collection of instruments.

And the words that create the sounds echoing from a soloist vocal cords.

I inspire writers to write songs,

producers to produce them and singers to sing them.

I make music possible. I cause songs to come alive.

I AM!

PLAYFUL, JOYFUL, EMOTIONAL, AND FREE!

I am proud to be a girl.

I am proud to be me!

I have lots and lots of personality!

I AM! HEALTH

I am as healthy as I eat.

When I feel sick, I remember that I am the fruit, vegetables, vitamins and all the other nutrients I eat from plants and gardens here on earth. (Psalm 104:14)

Its naturalness energizes me and gives me that perk.

But when I eat unhealthy,

I become the junk food and the sweets that are no good for me or my teeth.

That makes me feel stuffed, sluggish and awfully weak.

I am what I eat!

I AM! Drug Free

I do not use any form of drugs or medicine unless it is prescribed to me by my doctor or given to me by my parents or guardian.

I understand the danger of taking things that may not agree with my body and can cause me to become physically or mentally ill.

If my peers or anyone should offer me a drink that has alcohol in it or ask me if I'd like to take a puff (smoke), my answer will be no.

Smoking messes up my lungs and causes cancer and drinking can affect my liver. I am smart enough to know to stay away from things that can only harm me.

Once I am old enough to make my own decision on whether or not I will drink or smoke. How old I am will not take away the risk.

I don't need drugs to have fun.

Doing drugs doesn't make me cool and not doing drugs doesn't make me a nerd.

My name is _____ and I vow to keep my

mind, body and spirit free, by remaining drug free!

I AM! ATHLETIC

I go to the GYM, RUN, JUMP, EXCERCISE, LIFT WEIGHTS, PLAY SPORTS, enter BODY BUILDING CONTEST AND COMPETE.

I participate in the OLYMPICS.

I even WIN MEDALS & CHAMPIONSHIPS.

And because I BELIEVE in My ABILITIES, I WORK HARD and NEVER CHEAT.

I DRINK lots of WATER and WATCH what I EAT.

This is how I reach My GOALS, fullfill My ASPIRATIONS, ACHIEVE and COMPLETE.

I AM FIT, HEALTHY, AND DRUG FREE.

I AM an ATHLETE!

I AM!

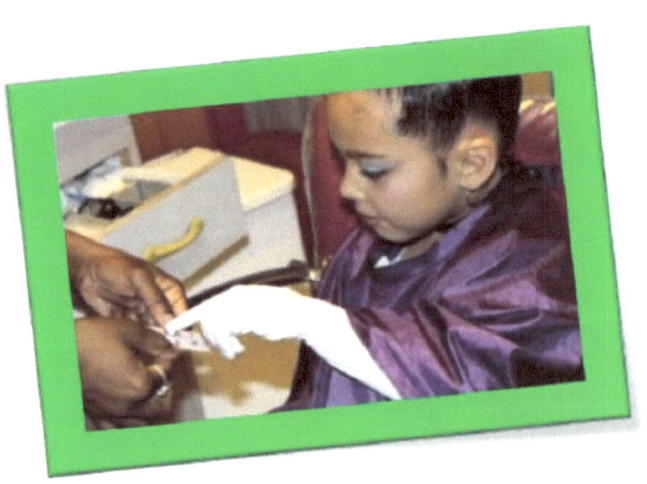

Well Groomed

I go to the SPA, HAIR SALON, or NAIL SHOP and get my HAIR, FEET, NAILS, FACE AND EYEBROWS done.

I AM fresh and clean.

This is the result of good personal hygiene.

I take showers to assure that my body doesn't smell.

So when others look at me, it is easy to tell.

I brush and floss my teeth whenever I eat,

in the morning and at night before I go to sleep.

I wash, brush, and comb my hair

so that dandruff doesn't accumulate and flare.

I use deodorant, perfume and body sprays

that cause others to stop and compliment me on how I smell amazed.

Inquiring the name of the fragrance I am wearing,

in conversation we become engaged.

I wash and clean my clothing so no stains are glowing.

I iron my clothing so no wrinkles are showing.

I lotion my body to keep my skin looking beautiful and moist,

dry skin isn't a good look or choice.

I AM!

A TREASURE BOX.

Like most GIRLS, if you open me up INSIDE you'll find lots and lots of hidden treasures like my gifts and talents, strengths and weaknesses, and even a few of my challenges and secrets.

I AM! SOCIAL

I interact and socialize with others. I am friendly.

I smile, wave or say hello to let others know that I am approachable (welcoming).

Though school is a place where I go to learn, it allows me to make new friends,

develop social skills; build relationships with peers (boys and girls), and other adults.

It also gives me an opportunity to become a part of a class, as well as an extracurricular activity.

When I am exposed to new people, places, and environments it helps me to grow,

learn and discover things about me.

I AM!
A GREAT FRIEND

I AM a cheerleader. I celebrate my BESTIE, and others' success and accomplishments.

I AM genuine. I am not phony, dishonest or spiteful.

I do not act one way with a certain group of people, and then act differently when they are no longer around. Neither do I pretend to be a person's friend in front of them, but talk behind their back, saying mean or bad things about them when they are not present.

I don't think it is nice, cute or funny when others do things intentionally to hurt or embarrass someone; then act as if it was a mistake.

I AM NOT judgmental. I do not judge or criticize others. I am careful about forming an opinion about others when I do not have all of the facts. If I judge, I too shall be judged. (Luke 6: 37)

I AM NOT an Instigator, Gossiper, Ringleader or Troublemaker. I AM a PEACEMAKER.

I don't go around talking about other people, spreading rumors or repeating what I hear that may or may not be true. I don't boost up fights or encourage arguments.

I don't carry "he say or she say" news back and forth between two people that don't get along or like each other or had a disagreement and are not speaking to one another as a result of it.

This doesn't help to resolve anything. In fact, it only makes the problem worse. In 1Timothy 5:13 of the Bible, persons who do this are called busy bodies. I do not wish to be labeled as this.

I AM an encourager. I possess power that empowers others. When I encourage others, I, too, am encouraged.

Every Girl Needs to Know Who She Is Not!

A Very Important Part of Knowing Who You Are Comes with Knowing Who You Are Not

SPEAK THESE THINGS ABOUT YOURSELF

I AM NOT an accident, mistake, or error. I am a blessing from God, and God does not make mistakes.

I AM NOT an afterthought. I am a before thought. I wasn't just put together; I was created. In the creation of me was lots of thought and planning.

I am a plan that is a part of the Master's plan.

I AM NOT a bad person. I sometimes make mistakes or poor choices. But with a little help, they can be corrected, and I am forgiven.

I AM NOT perfect. I may not always get it right the first time or even the second time. But I can always try again.

I AM NOT a victim. I am not here to be abused or misused by others. No one has the right to put their hands on me in any offensive or uncomfortable way.

Every touch, every hug, and every ounce of love shall be as innocent, peaceful, and harmless as a small, beautiful and gentle white dove.

I AM NOT necessarily a product of my environment or upbringing. So don't label me or place me inside of a box.

I AM NOT an "IT" or a "THING." I am a person with a name. My name is

_____.

POETICALLY SPEAKING:

I AM NOT!

THE AVERAGE GIRL.

I STILL BELIEVE IN DRESSES AND HIGH HEELS

AND CANDY CURLS.

I STILL LIKE HUGS AND KISSES

AND BEDTIME STORIES…

ALL THE LITTLE THINGS THAT

MIXES AND FIXES.

And there are two other MAJOR things **I AM NOT!**

I AM NOT a bully.

I do not take advantage of others because they are younger or smaller in size than I am. Neither do I use my strength nor connections (circle of friends or membership to a group or gang) to bully others.

There is nothing cool about bullying others or trying to make them afraid of me. Bullies are not strong; in fact, they are weak and lack empathy (care or concern) for others.

Some bullies possess low self-esteem; they try to pretend to be tough to make others think they have it all together.

But the sad truth is most bullies have been bullied, physically abused or mistreated by someone they love, trusted or thought was their friend and it is their way of dealing with the hurt or disappointment they feel.

Being bullied can be very embarrassing when it happens in front of peers. Just as it can be frightening when you are all alone and have no help.

Some girls have felt threatened or humiliated enough to ask their parent or guardian to change schools or move away.

Personally I don't think bullying looks good on girls. Not to say it looks good on anyone. Bullies are mean, bossy, ugly, stubborn, and obviously not so smart.

Girls' who carry themselves as ladies and know who they are uses their talents (skills), and intelligence (brain); not their fist to get what they want.

I AM NOT a boy.

Girls are different from boys in many ways:

Girls' bodies have things that boys do not have. Though boys' and girls' bodies go through stages and natural changes, as girls grow their bodies go through a monthly cleansing cycle that boys don't. It is called a Menstrual Cycle.

Usually around nine or ten years old, or maybe even a little bit older girls begin to hear and learn more about this cycle.

Girls are shaped differently from boys. Boys have their own sports, underwear, and clothing, and so do girls.

There is some specific clothing that girls wear that separate them from boys. Some of girls' clothing includes bras, panty hose, slips, girdles and panties.

These things help keep things in place and enhance girls' shapes and keep things from showing that shouldn't be.

Some girls, but not all girls, are known for wearing things like dresses or skirts, high heels, purses, nail polish, lip stick or lip gloss, and hair accessories.

But this is not true for the tomboy. This is the girl that prefers to wear sneakers, jeans or a pair of baggy sweat pants and a t-shirt. For her, comfort never hurts!

She doesn't care for the curls or all the fancy hairstyles like most girls. Simple suits her just fine!

She enjoys doing many of the same things that boys do. She appreciates sports, cars, and video games, and other activities that are less feminine.

She may choose staying at home to watch or play a game of football with the guys over shopping with the gals.

And because of that, it is often said that she acts, dresses or even looks like a boy. Yet, she is still very much a girl, considering everything else that makes her a girl, and not a boy.

Boys are masculine (strong, brave, men). As boys grow, they develop facial hair around their lips (mustache) and chin (beard).

Girls are feminine (sensitive, gentle, women). Females can become pregnant and have babies, but males cannot. Boys are male. Girls are female.

Every Girl Needs to Belong

A Major Part of Knowing Who You Are Comes With Knowing Whose You Are And Why?
WHOSE ARE YOU?

I AM Somebody! **I AM** a child of the King.

I was created and given an identity, shape, and form long before I was born from my mother's womb. (Jeremiah 1: 5)

I AM Chosen. "Greatness" is upon me and it lives on the inside of me. I have the DNA (qualities and characteristics) to prove it.

I AM Royalty! 1 Peter 2: 9-10 describes me as such.

I AM like clay in HIS hands, and each day HE takes me, holds me, and breathes on me.

I AM being molded, shaped, and made new. (Isaiah 64: 8)

I AM a Queen. I have a father in heaven that watches over me. He will never fall out of love with me or deny me.

He will never tell me to do anything that is wrong or that I will later regret.

All I have to do is call to Him when I am in trouble, and He will rescue me. He promised to never leave me. (Deuteronomy 31:6)

And because of this promise **I BELIEVE** He will be with me until the end of my journey.

I AM! FAITH

**WITHOUT FAITH IT IS IMPOSSIBLE TO PLEASE GOD.
(Hebrews 11: 6)**

That is why I walk by faith, and not by sight. I know that things aren't always what it look like.

And because I believe God will deliver. I thank Him in advance (before I receive) what I ask for.

SPEAK THESE THINGS BY FAITH

I AM protected. **I AM** provided for.

Therefore, I will not fret (worry) about any lack of anything such as, food, clothing, shelter or money. Neither will I concern myself about any evil (bad) or harm intentions toward me.

I AM never alone. God is with me. God is for me. He stands alongside me in my greatest battles and fears.

I AM not too young to believe. I have dreams of doing and becoming someone great just as anyone else.

I AM not too young to set goals. In fact it is a good time for me to start.

I BELIEVE God want to bless me.

I BELIEVE it is His heart's desire for me to be happy.

I AM confident that I am who God says I am, and **I WILL** go forth and do great things.

I AM determined to keep the faith even when everyone and everything surrounding me appear to be faithless.

I KNOW if I do my part, I can depend on God to do the rest.

I AM!

Love is God. Love is me.

Love is the shade that exists up under every tree.

Love is life. Life is love.

It is the sun, moon and stars that gazes from above.

If I love you and you love me,

We can change the world and our community.

It is love that makes us one big happy family,

Love is Unity!

And because I AM Loved, God uses people like my parents or guardians, teachers, elders and sometimes even strangers to correct me when I am wrong. (1 Peter 4:8)

Those adults may become upset with me for my actions, and scream, yell or maybe even punish me.

But I remember that they too are not perfect.

For some adults it is their way of saying, I love you, and I only want what is best.

Correction is a form of love and with love sometimes come consequences.

When I am corrected, I am being shown love.

I know this because in the Bible, Proverbs 3:12 says, "For whom the Lord loves he corrects."

For it is through loving correction that I AM being made perfect!

I will not recognize (accept) anything other than love because I know who I am and whose I am.

And because I am an expression of Love, it is my responsibility to walk in love and humility.

Yet, when others make it hard for me to love them, I have the option of loving them at a distance.

And there is one other MAJOR thing **I AM!**

I AM a LADY!

I act like a lady, walk like a lady, talk like a lady and dress like a lady.

I do not sit with my feet, knees, or any parts of my legs in a chair. I sit with my legs crossed, especially when I am wearing a dress or a skirt.

I wear things that are appropriate and not too short or too tight that they reveal things that are private and should remain tucked, sealed, out of sight.

By carrying myself in such way, I command respect.

I do not use, answer or react to names or words that degrade me as a young lady. I have self-respect.

I do not allow rude or disrespectful behaviors or acts of young men who have not yet been taught how to treat or speak to a lady to define who I am.

Such lady-like actions will cause young men to want to open doors for me, pull out chairs for me, and help me up and down the stairs.

It will also cause them to call me by my name and no other rude or disrespectful name.

I am becoming the type of young lady whose lady-like actions are so impressive that nice young men will want to ask me out on dates and maybe even buy me chocolate milk shakes!

I'm on my way to becoming that virtuous woman that Proverbs 31 in the Bible portrays.

I AM! Michelliah McCraney

the Author of this book, and "I Exist!" because inside of me is God; bits and pieces of YOU. (1 John 4: 4)

THE END!

Michelliah McCraney is a mother, grandmother, educator, mentor, inspirational speaker, and spoken word artist. She is also the Founder and Executive Director of Aspiring Beautiful & Confident Girls, Inc.

Ms. McCraney was born and raised in South Florida. She has worked in Florida's public school system in Miami-Dade, Broward and Alachua county using her skills to enhance the lives of children and families in need.

Throughout her 21-year tenure, Ms. McCraney has worked with Head Start, Pre-K and elementary school children. The children she has worked with include Exceptional Student Education (ESE), Attention Deficit Hyperactivity Disorder (ADHD), Attention Deficit Disorder (ADD) and those diagnosed with Autism Spectrum Disorder (ASD). As a Behavior Research Teacher (BRT), she successfully transformed the behavior of many challenging students.

Advancing in her career, Ms. McCraney administered the Parent Resource Center and various after school programs, arranged Career Day programs, organized Youth Mentoring Programs, and implemented Parenting Workshops. In addition, she built partnerships with local businesses throughout the community to support incentive programs for students and families in need.

Embracing her gifts, Ms. McCraney wrote and produced her first Poetry CD in 2010, after which she carried out her vision of writing and publishing her very own curriculum to mentor and teach young girls.

Accepting her purpose, what was only intended to be one book became a three-part series with a matching journal.

www.ingramcontent.com/pod-product-compliance
Lightning Source LLC
LaVergne TN
LVHW072053070426
835508LV00002B/73
9780999810130